tree of life

m. lانz 5/96

MOMENTS
OF
SILENCE

BY JOHN COLUMBUS TAYLOR

WITH AFFIRMATIONS BY
LOUISE L. HAY

HAY HOUSE, INC.
CARSON, CA

MOMENTS OF SILENCE
by John Columbus Taylor

The author of this book does not dispense medical advice nor prescribe the use of any technique as a form of treatment for physical or medical problems without the advice of a physician, either directly or indirectly. The intent of the author is only to offer information of a general nature to help you in your quest for physical fitness and good health. In the event you use any of the information in this book for yourself, which is your constitutional right, the author and the publisher assume no responsibility for your actions.

Library of Congress Cataloging-in-Publication Data

Taylor, John Columbus, 1947–
    Moments of silence / by John Columbus Taylor, with affirmations by
  Louise L. Hay
      p.   cm.
    ISBN 1–56170–071–1 : $15.00
    1. Self-actualization (Psychology) 2. Affirmations. I. Hay,
  Louise L. II. Title
BF637.S4T394   1993   93–17948
158'.12—dc20   CIP

Library of Congress Catalog Card No. 93–17948
ISBN: 1–56170–071–1

"Tree of Life"
Pen and Ink Drawing by Monica Lanz.

Internal design by David Butler
Typesetting by Freedmen's Organization, Los Angeles, CA 90004

93 94 95 96 97 98   10 9 8 7 6 5 4 3 2 1
First Printing, August 1993

Published and Distributed in the United States by:

Hay House, Inc.
P.O. Box 6204
Carson, CA 90749-6204

Printed in the United States of America
on Recycled Paper

DEDICATION

This book is dedicated to all of you who are looking for answers. Your questions about life and why it is the way it is are an integral part of the energy that assists the answers to come forth in some way. The messages here are one way in which those answers are made available.

I want to acknowledge and express my deepest gratitude to Sharon Huffman without whose encouragement this book may not have been created. During my own times of questioning, doubt, and stress, she was the coach that kept me moving forward. I want to thank Shari who always believed in me in spite of some of the appearances. I want to thank Linda, Peggy, Kathy, Candace, Sheri, Gail, Greg, Dave, Roger, Patty, Amos, Barbara, Laura, Caren, Patricia, Emily, and Robyn for their friendship, support and so much more. I thank my mom and dad who had the patience and love to bring five wonderful children into the world. This book is also dedicated to them and to others, seen and unseen, who have assisted my growth and learning.

Finally, I want to thank Louise Hay for the love and the courage to allow me this opportunity to present to you a work of love that may be different and challenging to some, but hopefully inspiring to all in your search for understanding. May you all be blessed to find what you seek.

—John Columbus Taylor

FOREWORD

Life is wonderful. And I have learned that whatever I need to know is revealed to me. And whoever I need to meet is brought to me. Recently life has brought me John Columbus Taylor and I am deeply grateful.

How many times we have searched for answers only to have them elude us? We know there is an infinite wisdom in the universe and we would all like to tap into it. Some people seem to be more connected to their center of inner wisdom than others. John Columbus Taylor is one of the more connected ones. When he sits down to ask questions beautiful answers come flowing out of his consciousness.

My own inner being resonates with the substance of this information. It is clear and pure. Much of it is very deep. We will not always understand or agree with all of it immediately. Yet as we grow in understanding we will see the wisdom in each sentence.

So this is a book to keep by your bed or favorite chair, to pick up daily and open it where you will. The message will be perfect for you at that time. Read the open page. Allow yourself to absorb the information. Then take the affirmation and let it run through your mind for the rest of the day. Or take it into sleep with you. If you do this daily, by the end of a year your own inner wisdom will be flowing.

Each of us wishes to increase our own understanding

of life and the many issues involved. The wisdom in this book is here to stimulate you into awakening to the great resources of your own being. You already have all the answers within you. If John and I can, by offering this book, help you to connect with your own resource center, then we are very pleased indeed, and our work is well done.

May we all continue to grow in understanding and may our lives be filled with an abundance of all good in every area.

You are loved.

—Louise L. Hay

INTRODUCTION

There have been times in my life when I experienced challenge and crisis. A few years ago I began to go out into the country away from the noise and distractions to a place where I could simply sit by a tree and think. Somehow just being in nature had a very calming effect.

I began to ask questions, not just about what I was going through, but about many aspects of life. To my delight and surprise, even in those most trying times, I found a connection within to words of wisdom and encouragement. Periodic retreats away from the stresses of daily life have become a necessary part of my experience.

I started taking pencil and paper with me on these journeys. The information that I received from within was often very specific. At other times the words were poetic and timeless in their simplicity and beauty. The purpose of this book is to share with you part of that wisdom which has meant so much to me.

We all perhaps experience times in our lives when there seem to be no answers, when the challenges and difficulties are almost unbearable. Yet when I experienced those low moments, there were words and suggestions that came from within to guide and direct me to greater joy and happiness. My desire is that these words might inspire you to connect with your own great source of inspiration and understanding within.

—John Columbus Taylor

TABLE OF CONTENTS

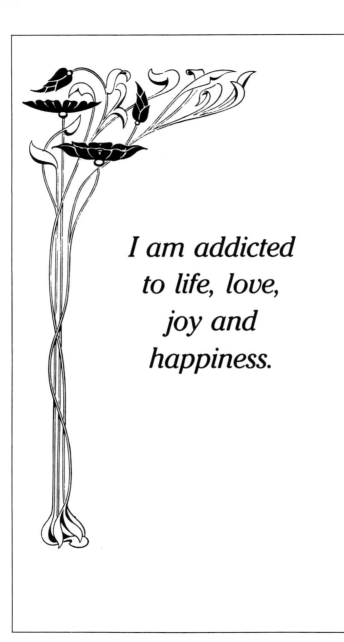

*I am addicted
to life, love,
joy and
happiness.*

ADDICTIONS

*A*ddictions are the result of living in fear and anger. They are your mind's attempt to deny what you are really thinking and feeling. In repressing the emotions you only delay the very healing you so desperately seek. The substances or experiences you use to repress feeling are only substitutes for the love and joy your heart and soul really want.

When you begin to love yourself, you will discover that real joy and happiness comes from using your creativity to express love and compassion for your brothers and sisters. There are many who stand willing to assist when you are ready to heal. The choice to heal is worth the effort required.

If you want to be free from addictions, you must first have the courage to face the fear and anger you have been denying. Realize that the fear is your own creation. And it is impossible for the creation to be more powerful than its creator. Then allow those who are friends to help, and let your only addictions be to life, love, joy, and happiness.

15

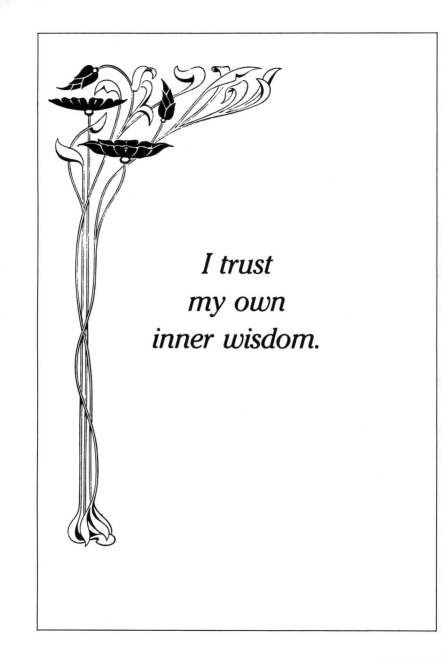

*I trust
my own
inner wisdom.*

ADVICE

You seek advice from others because you do not hear the truth in your own being that speaks from the depths of your heart and soul. Yet how can you hear your own wisdom with all the noise of confusion and fear you make? Your mind is often so preoccupied with the illusions of life that you have lost touch with your heart.

Heed not others' advice, though they mean well, for they do not know your deepest thoughts and desires. Their perspective of you is clouded by their own fears, and they cannot even advise themselves. But if they would be your friends, let them share only their differing perspective, not in terms of advice, but in providing you an additional awareness of choices available on your path.

Do not hurry a decision in fear or anger, for in quiet and in the fullness of time your choice shall be made plain by your own inner wisdom. The greatest advice to which you can adhere is to take not others' advice, but ultimately just your own.

*I am always
the perfect age
and radiate
eternal youth.*

AGING

One of your greatest fears is growing old. That fear has reached such an intensity that you hasten it rather than heal it. Instead of hating yourself for growing older, give thanks for the wrinkles of maturity. It shows the beauty and wisdom gained from living life fully, and the joy in finding the meaning of love.

If you try out of desperation to hang onto your youth, the emotional stress only hastens the wrinkles. Take time in quiet to envision yourself as whole and in a state of well-being. Your power of imagination is a greater gift than you realize. If you are constantly in front of a mirror looking for signs of aging, you will surely find them. But if you spend your time experiencing the joy that life can bring, you will not have time for worry, and you will retain a more youthful appearance. The wrinkles from love and laughter are rarely permanent, but always beautiful.

*I lovingly allow
my life to be
as it is and
others to be
who they are.*

ALLOWING

To allow is to express the highest of love. No greater love can be expressed by one than to allow all which exists merely to be as it chooses to be. To allow is to serve no indictment. To allow is to pass no judgment. You would not be where you are now if you could truly live this. You have been allowed by life to be where you are. When you have this in your understanding, you will have taken one of the greatest steps you'll ever know.

There is no polarity of right or wrong in allowing. Each soul is his own master, and must find truth in his own time. And that truth is relative.

The futility of anger creates hatred. The futility of condemnation creates disease. The futility of judgment creates war. But to allow is to love in the very highest possible essence of love itself. And in this does life have meaning and purpose, for it is the meaning and the purpose. It is love.

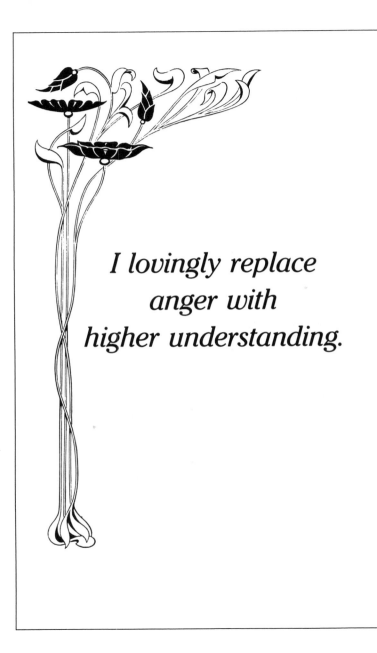

*I lovingly replace
anger with
higher understanding.*

Patrick Eric Yarosh
3-6-74 ∞ 5-16-93

ANGER

When you truly become as a master, you will no longer need the escape of anger. To hold onto anger as you do now is to accumulate a poison within that does not dissipate in time.

Anger is a denial in the mind of the heart's prodding to have compassion and forgiveness for what you see of yourself in others. What you understand and can forgive in another, you have been and have forgiven in yourself. What causes you anger is your lesson of the moment and a glimpse into your own being. Allow the anger to be for its lesson, for to deny it is only to deny a part of yourself. In the twinkling of an eye you can remove from within the poison of anger by seeking its higher understanding. And you do that in unconditional love to yourself and to your brother. Then the energy of anger can be used as determined motivation to accomplish what you desire to do.

*My attitude of love
and compassion
creates a
beautiful world.*

ATTITUDES

*A*ttitudes and feelings empower thought into the manifestation of reality. Attitudes are the spiritual harmonic filter through which being is expressed, and through which one's creations are perceived.

To those who have the attitude of love and compassion, the world is a most marvelous and beautiful experience. And life gives back to them their just increase of who they are. To those who have the attitude of fear and hatred, who condemn and judge without first knowing and who sadly cannot know because of their fears, to them life equally reflects back their perception of themselves. Their attitude thus becomes so dark that it allows no light to shine forth from the center of their being.

Yet the destiny of all is to know their divinity. And each must accept the responsibility that thoughts and feelings are one's own creation. All have the power and the right at any moment to choose what they shall think or feel. For it is not the circumstance which creates the feeling, but rather the thought which creates the circumstance.

*I accept
my radiant
beauty
within.*

BEAUTY

Beauty is the essence of being, and everyone is beautiful. You miss that essence when you judge from your own limited perspectives. Do not judge from appearances, for all life possesses beauty because it dwells in eternity, and not just in your mind.

A flower is beautiful in its simplicity of being. It does not need you to be what it is. A child is beautiful in its carefree play, and is thus a great teacher for you. A star is beautiful in its nighttime splendor as it gently bathes the evening in twinkles of light. It speaks to you of your own eternal beauty and splendor. There is beauty even in death for it is the walking through a door into greater light and love, joy and peace.

Beauty is not just in the eye of the beholder. As you allow yourself to see the beauty in life, you recognize and accept the beauty within. Then your own beauty will shine forth as a radiant star.

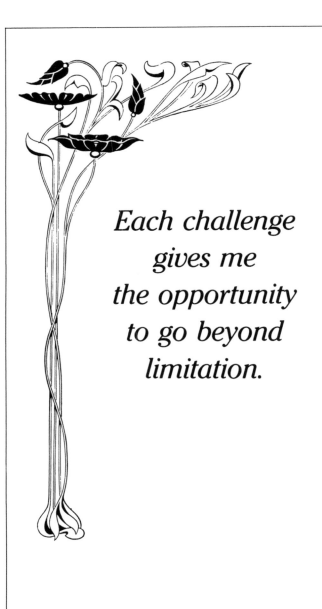

*Each challenge
gives me
the opportunity
to go beyond
limitation.*

CHALLENGES

You often face seemingly impossible tasks. They are there to teach you that all things are possible in the unlimitedness of life. Your accomplishment of these tasks stretches you to a greater awareness of your abilities through the love of life.

Greet each challenge as a blessing, for it speaks that you are ready for growth. Even in apparent failure there is success, for you learn of behaviors that do not produce what you desire. Judge not the outcome of the task, nor your own performance of it. See instead the beauty in understanding as you steadily grow in your awareness of the universe. Give thanks for challenges. They are your soul's desire to be free of limitation.

I easily go through change with poise and grace.

CHANGE

*C*hange in your life is the indicator of growth at the deeper levels of your being. You often desire change and even ask for it, but fear it when it comes. You live now in a time of great change simply because humanity is experiencing much spiritual growth. Rather than fear or resist change, welcome it with open arms. It is a gift from life and the precursor of greater happiness and freedom.

To change your experience of life, you must change your attitudes and beliefs about life. This is an inner process. The external reality is a reflection of your inner self and the beliefs that you are living. As you expand in consciousness, your beliefs about the world change. As your beliefs change, your experiences in life change.

Do not get caught up in the whirlwind of the external changes and events taking place. Seek within the solid foundation of knowing who you really are. In the calm and peace of inner knowing you can more easily go through the times of change with poise and grace. In so doing, you can be a light of love and understanding to humanity during this wonderful time of rapid expansion, growth, and change. And you will emerge from the process with a clearer remembrance of your own divinity.

*I am a playful child
of the universe
and I am
special and loved.*

CHILDREN

Your children are your greatest teachers. Honor them and give thanks for the blessing that they are, for through them you are shown the way to a more joyful life. You do injustice to yourselves by disallowing their being. You cannot shape or mold them, for they have already chosen who they are to be. Have you forgotten? You also are a child. Be about the business of children.

And how may you become as a child? It is found in your faith and trust in the universe, and not in your intellect and materiality. You lost that faith and trust when you became more concerned with fear and when you became the judge of all around you.

The child that you were loved without condition. The child that you were played with life. The child that you were created joy in each moment, and would have continued to do so if it had not been taught limitation and fear, if it had not been judged and condemned.

Allow yourself to become a child again, and to experience the joy in just being. Seek within in the quiet of each moment that special purpose in life for you. And know that as a divine child of the universe you are special and loved, no matter what form your place may assume. For life created you in its own loving cradle.

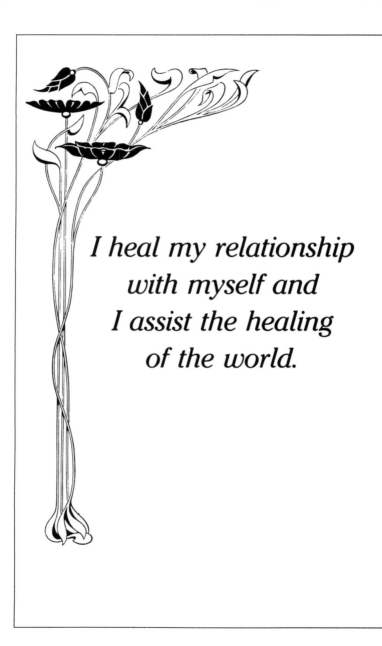

*I heal my relationship
with myself and
I assist the healing
of the world.*

COMMUNITY

The need to belong creates the existence of communities. You want to be with other people who think and feel as you do, who have similar values and goals. Nations exist as an extension of a larger set of values and goals. But you all belong to the community of humanity. As such you have a responsibility to see the value in all life upon the planet, as well as human life. You must learn to see your differences, not as problems, but as opportunities to expand the possibilities for your individual lives, and to expand your ability to express love.

There is a great need now to heal the differences that have caused you to be combative and competitive. Many of the challenges you face can be solved only through global cooperation. International and interracial relationships become much more important because of the speed with which evolution and technology are advancing, and because of the risks posed by improper stewardship of global resources. Independence is a wonderful quality that must be balanced with the recognition that you still live on the same piece of dirt moving through space. What you do affects everyone else, and what they do affects you. You are far more connected with all life than you realize.

The success of these larger relationships depends on the relationship you have with yourself. Heal that, and the relationships of communities and nations will also be healed.

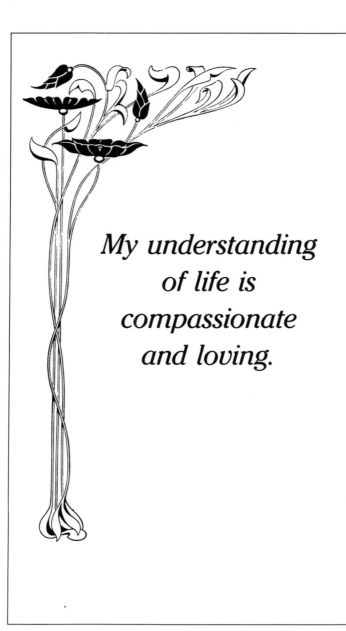

*My understanding
of life is
compassionate
and loving.*

COMPASSION

ompassion is the love from an understanding heart in seeing in another what it has known in itself. Compassion does not express pity, for in pity it is immobilized to tears. It does not express grief, for in grief it stagnates to inaction. Nor does it express regret, for it knows the beauty of growth.

Compassion *allows*, as does life, for in allowing is the higher experience of love. The more you know of your brothers and sisters, the more you see yourself in the mirrors that life brings. The deeper your feeling of compassion, the more you have found forgiveness within, and the more profound, yet simple is your understanding of life. For in compassion you are assured a place in the loving heart of eternity.

*I seek greater
understanding
during crisis.*

CRISIS

The purpose of crisis is the surrender of the ego to accept the reality of a greater part of yourself. For too long you have denied your divinity. You have ignored the lessons in life, and you have refused to accept your real power in thought and feeling. The crisis forces you to look deeper within to find the power to solve the problem.

Crises occur as a wake-up call from your heart and soul that you are living out of harmony with life and its principles. It is one of the ways that life forces you to seek greater understanding. During the vulnerable moments of a crisis, you are more likely to be humble and willing to listen and learn. You know that you have learned if the crisis does not repeat itself. However, if you are experiencing repetitive patterns of difficulty, then it is a warning that you have been too rigid and dogmatic somewhere in your consciousness. Are you willing now to surrender to the love within?

*I am divine
and my life
is eternal.*

DEATH

Death, and even birth, are but the opening of a door, and life is but the pause in the room between. How great is the sunshine on a summer's day outside the door of your room. How much greater then is the light beyond the door you call death. Fear not the door, but that which keeps you from its opening.

What you think you see as an end is the reality of a new beginning. What you think has passed from your presence has merely assumed a higher level of service and being. And what you hold in sadness and grief is instead the eternity of truth, peace, joy, and love.

You fear death because of attachment to things that possess you. You fear death because your identity of self is merely as a physical body. And you fear life because of the limitation of time.

Death is not a thing to fear, nor is it an end. Death is the beginning of a new eternity, just as is each new moment in life. So live each moment with which you are blessed in loving service to your brothers and sisters. You are divine and your life is eternal in the faith and trust of love. For death is only an illusion, but the life that you are is now and forever.

I owe no one
and I am free.

DEBT

The need to borrow and be in debt is a result of the spoiled inner child who selfishly says, *"I want what I want when I want it!"* You have a great power within to create. But want and desire must be coupled with patience and wisdom. Otherwise, in your indebtedness you no longer feel free to make unrestricted and loving choices for yourself. The anxiety around debt blocks your creativity and imagination.

Debt has enslaved most of the people in the world. It contributes to disease and war. True security does not come from money and possessions, but from the wisdom to recognize what is truly important and what one really needs, and from the patience to allow life to bring it to you in its own perfect timing. Owe no one, and freedom will be yours. And when you finally learn how to give without conditions, your receiving will be the same.

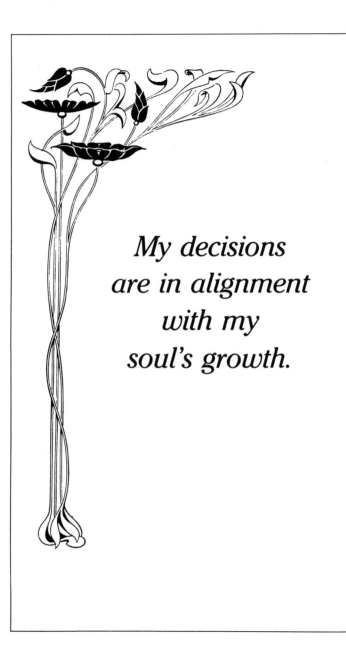

*My decisions
are in alignment
with my
soul's growth.*

DECISIONS

When you are faced with a choice, listen to the urging of your heart in its desire to create from love the greatest good for all. There are times when the choice may seem difficult because it presents many challenges. Those challenges are there for your growth, and for others with whom you share life's experience.

Do not always choose the easy path, for its complacent way stagnates the soul. Have the courage to choose growth, though at times it may lead to pain, for it opens the door to compassion and understanding. Have the courage to choose challenge, though its spices are tart and sweet, for in it does life thrive and find wisdom. Have the courage to choose truth, though you marvel at its many revelations, for each master has a story to tell of the glimpses into the eternity of his being. And have the courage to choose love, though you are humbled in its presence, for in humility shall you taste of the essence of life which is love.

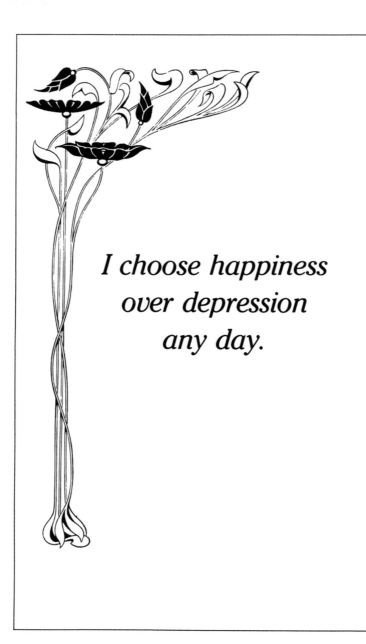

*I choose happiness
over depression
any day.*

DEPRESSION

Depression is the feeling of loss. You feel depression whenever something leaves your life for which you had an attachment or to which you had an ego identification. Repressed anger often becomes depression because you have unconsciously lost self-respect and integrity. In denying the feeling of anger, you have not been honest with yourself.

To heal depression you must learn to release attachments. One of the easiest ways to release attachments is to realize that nothing ever leaves your life unless something better is on the way. You don't have to know exactly what it is or how it will manifest, or even when. You only need to feel the childlike, joyful and trusting innocence and anticipation that is already within you.

Sometimes the purpose of loss is to get people to see where they have become attached to someone or something as if that were the source of their happiness. Happiness is an inherent part of your nature. It does not depend on external conditions. You can choose at any moment to feel happy. But in the process of choosing what you want to feel, do not deny the real feelings that are there. That is what you have been doing for far too long. You will feel much happier and you will free yourself from depression much more quickly by being honest with yourself and with others.

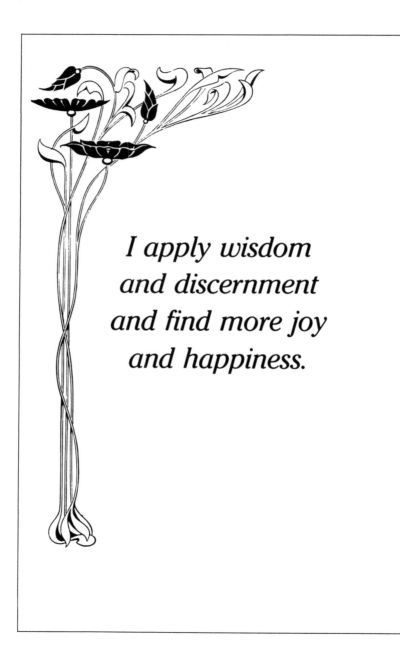

*I apply wisdom
and discernment
and find more joy
and happiness.*

DISCERNMENT

Discernment is the application of insight and perception. It is a necessary quality for your evolution. In your growth, be open and receptive to the possibilities for greater joy and happiness. But do not be so open that you become gullible.

Do not believe everything you see and hear. Test it with your own inner wisdom.

Do not become doubting or cynical. You risk becoming embittered, which is difficult to resolve. You have many possibilities for miracles, but they happen more often when you are joyful and loving rather than angry or cynical.

Do not buy into another's promise of great fortune. Let the ideas for your own greatness be revealed from within.

Mastery begins by being honest with yourself about your experiences and the beliefs those experiences have created. Whatever your beliefs have created, it is time to be receptive to new options. When you become aware of a greater possibility for yourself, it may take time before the old limited beliefs change. Give yourself that time to stretch and change. Be discerning of anything another person says. Pay attention to your feelings. Watch out for those areas where you are needy or attached. That is where you are most likely to be deceived. Apply the wisdom already within, and you will be gently led beyond your limitations to more joy, aliveness and love.

49

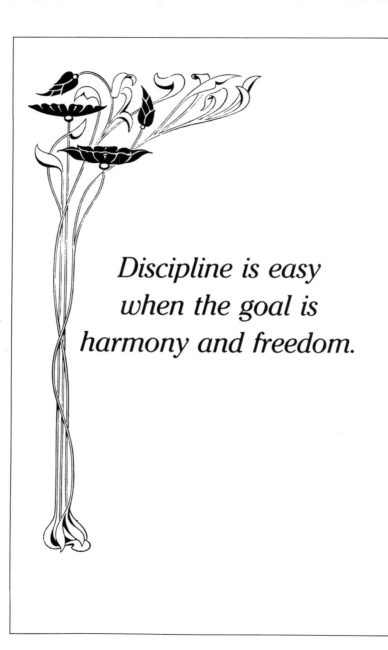

*Discipline is easy
when the goal is
harmony and freedom.*

DISCIPLINE

Discipline is the adherence to a set of principles of behavior. Great achievements are accomplished by great masters who are focused and disciplined in their approach. Any pathway of mastery requires persistence, consistency, determination and discipline.

As a child you were disciplined when you disobeyed. As you mature, life will also discipline you if you do not follow and apply its laws correctly. The laws of life are operating all the time, whether you are aware of them or not. Few of humanity have grown sufficiently at the conscious level to fully understand those laws. With discipline comes structure, harmony and freedom. Once you learn the rules of the game, it's a lot more fun to play.

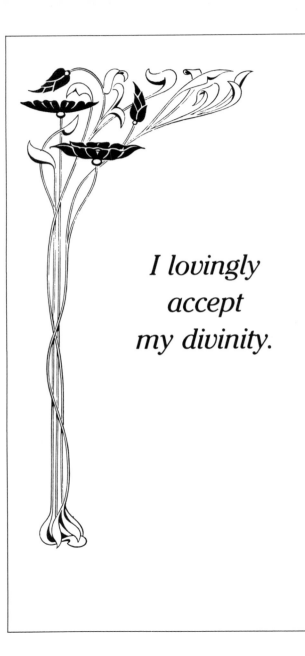

*I lovingly
accept
my divinity.*

DIVINITY

Your divinity is the reality of you that you have denied and forgotten for ages. It is the heritage that connects you to eternal life. You are special and loved, as are all the children of the universe. Even the lowliest in the rank of life, though they touch only a single soul in love, shall rock the foundations of eternity. For in the single expression of their love do they lift the harmony in all creation by living and giving the gift of their own love and divinity.

With your divinity comes great power, yet not in dominion over another, but in the understanding of who you are. And in the finding of truth comes divine humility, with love and compassion for all. For the wheat fields stand tall when the husks are empty, but lovingly bow to the earth in the fullness of their maturity.

*I have the ability
to make my dreams
come true.*

DREAMS

While you sleep, dreams are your connection to other realities, visits to the past or future, and suggestions for other ways to see life. They are symbols of where you may be in evolution, and the working out of the challenges you face during the day. Look for the symbols and hints your dreams contain to help you understand your life. A wealth of wisdom is contained in a dream.

Daydreams are unrealized desires awaiting your power to create. They are messages from your heart and soul of greater possibilities. Do not let your hopes and aspirations slip away as if they were impossible. Your soul aspires to bring you much greater joy and happiness if you would only take the time to connect with its guidance. The feeling of joy is one of its primary signals that you are on your correct path. And with that perfect guidance, you can be the genie who makes your dreams come true.

*I have faith in
the unlimited
loving power
of the universe.*

FAITH

Faith is creative thought. It is the knowing within that having the thought of a joyful desire means it is already on your pathway. It is the recognition of your oneness and reliance with all life. Through faith, your heart conceives good for the elevation of all.

Faith and trust are like a child at play, knowing its needs are always met without struggle or striving. Faith is the alignment and focus of the power that moves mountains when all else has failed. Faith is the ideal in a single acorn of the loving vision of its spreading bower to be.

Let go of your fears and limitations. Through faith you know you are loved. With faith each moment is an opportunity to create a wonderful and beautiful new life through the unlimited loving power of the universe.

I have a healthy relationship with my family.

FAMILY

The cause of family problems is the need to control rather than accept and allow. If you love and value yourself, and have a sense of your own identity, you will not feel threatened by another's disapproval. You realize that they can only approve of what they love and accept in themselves. Whatever they judge is often what they most fear.

Family is an important foundation upon which other relationships are built. Your immediate family—brothers, sisters, father and mother—represent the opportunity to learn and practice healthy and loving relationships. If you can make your family relationships more healthy, you carry this with you into all areas of your life. Strive to have the highest and most loving relationships you can with your family. The application of love will heal the differences. To apply love means that each member allows the others to be as they choose to be.

Many of you only consider blood relatives as your family. There is a greater family which must be considered: the family of humanity and all life on this planet. You are much more interdependent than you have considered. You cannot carelessly destroy any part of life, because your own life and the continuation of the species of humanity is enhanced by the successful continuation of all species of life. Love all life on the planet as if it were your own. It is.

*I let go of fear
and move forward
into a life of love.*

FEAR

Fear is an emotion that you have allowed to control you rather than use to avoid danger. You fear not having enough money. You fear not having enough time. You fear that you are not attractive and loved because you view yourself in comparison to others. You fear war, disease, and death, and in the process create them. If you focus on fear, you are feeding your life energy into its creation. You have forgotten that you are a loving, compassionate, imaginative, and perfect child of the universe, endowed eternally with power, divinity, and love.

You are where you are because of your fears. One of the great lessons of the human experience is that fear is your own creation. You must use the power of love to rise above it. Then create a reality founded in love, not only for yourself, but for all life. The time has come to let go of fear and move forward.

*I am flexible
and willing
to change.*

FLEXIBILITY

Flexibility is the willingness to adapt and to move through change with poise and grace. It is the ability to move and bend with the requirements of the moment without a stubborn fixation on what has to be. You live in times of rapid change and growth. If you are too rigid in your approach to life or unwilling to flow and change, there is the risk of breakdown. You are awakening to a greater understanding of truth and spiritual principle. If you hold on too tightly to what you thought was truth in the past, then you risk losing the opportunity to experience greater truths that can make your life easier and more joyful.

Just as the seed is softened with water so that it may burst forth into the light as a living plant, so too does your understanding and awareness soften your beliefs about life that you may become more than what you presently think yourself to be. Resistance to change only makes life harsh and difficult. Life exists because of growth and change, not in spite of it. Remain supple and flexible in your view of life, and it will bless you with greater freedom and happiness. Are you ready and willing to grow?

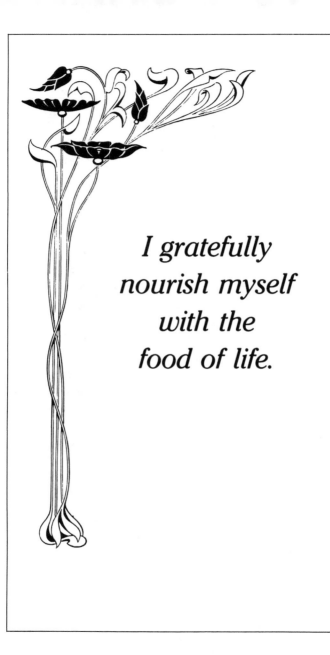

*I gratefully
nourish myself
with the
food of life.*

FOOD

Eat of life that you may live. How can that which is dead nourish the living? For life gives unto life, and the dead to death. When you kill that which lives, thinking for the purpose of eating only, you taste of death. When you bless the greatest of sacrifices, then you feed upon the sustenance of forever, the light of love itself. Then also you give back life to life.

The blessing of a crumb of bread gives back to you more of life than the feasts of kings and queens. It is not the what, but the how. Therein lies the answer. Not the revelling of gluttonous fools, but the humble thanksgiving of a grateful heart. To those who are humble, all is alive, and all is to be revered. Their food is the light, and its gift is eternal life.

*I lovingly forgive
myself and others,
and life forgives
and loves me.*

FORGIVENESS

To forgive is to presuppose a judgment. To judge is to presume a power you do not have. Can you now create a tree, direct the wind, or brighten a star? Then do not presume that which you have not become. Judge not, and you find there is no thing which requires your forgiveness. The grace of life has granted you that already. Only allow and observe, then you shall live in truth.

The only one needing forgiveness from you is you, for you are the creator of your reality in all its manifestations. When you accept and understand that responsibility, you shall find great release from the burdens of fear and limitation. Then you begin to create from the love of all life, and not just from what you presume must be forgiven. And you will know you have always had the forgiveness you seek because life has allowed you to be as you choose.

*I find my freedom
in love and truth.*

FREEDOM

*Y*ou have always been free, yet in your own mind you are imprisoned. Your thoughts often go no higher than yesterday's regret or tomorrow's fear. Freedom exists only in the now within.

The bumblebee is free because it succumbs not to limitation. The eagle can soar for it heeds no dread of heights. A child is free in its carefree play, for it knows that its needs are always met. Even the encrusted barnacle, fixed forever to some shoreline rock, fears not that the ocean will dry up or fail to give of its nutrients.

Your own freedom may be measured, not by thoughts of loftiness, but by the absence of limited thought. Do not give consideration to concepts of fear or limitation. Think only of love and truth, and you shall live in freedom. For in thoughts of fear, the watchman is more imprisoned than the one behind bars.

*I lovingly allow
my friends
to be.*

FRIENDS

*L*et any who would call themselves a friend listen only to your heart, and give service to your understanding. Those who in self-righteousness would feign unsolicited advice are not your friends. Those who would cause you to become dependent seek only to enslave. Those who lavishly ply you with gifts seek your indebtedness, for they are not even their own friends. And those whose lips speak lies upon your absence shall perish in their own grief.

Let your friends be those who share with you the truth and wisdom of the ages, but do not use them as weapons. Let your friends be those who give to your prosperity, and not to your seeming lack or limitations. Let your friends be those who assist you in your healing, for then they also heal themselves. Let your friends be those who simply allow you to be, with no judgment and no shame. And let them nurture your growth in its own appointed time, rather than cause you to be what you are not. And when you find those who are these things, treasure them and be their friend as well.

*I give in love
and I receive
in love.*

GIVING

When you give to another, let it be without condition or expectation. Let the reward be in the giving itself, and not in anticipated expressions of gratitude. And when others desire to give to you, do not deny them their expression of love within, but give thanks to life in the silence of your own being. For the giver is the greater receiver, and the receiver the greater giver in the constant flow of life.

Let your giving be from a thankful heart, and in the humble acceptance that you have grown to allow more love to express through you. Let your receiving likewise be in silent gratitude, for what you have given has returned to you increased.

Whatever goes out from you in word, thought, or deed returns with the same feeling in which it was sent. And it is better that you give to the heart of ten than the mind of ten thousand.

*My goal is
to know and
love myself.*

GOALS

ou often seek to obtain some material desire or goal. Yet real success and the true goal or purpose in life is in the discovery and knowing of yourself. For what do you have when a material goal is realized but an emptiness that must be satisfied by setting another goal?

What a price you pay when you seek only what you can touch with your hand or eye! What success have those who gather gold to themselves, only to break from its weight? What have those who direct the masses, only to drown in the sorrow of tears and hatred? And what have those who in their own glory have no friends and die alone?

When you live for the awareness of all the possibilities life holds for you, all desires and goals take their appointed place and manifest in a more perfect timing. Love yourself enough to allow more joyful possibilities. See the miracles happening in the universe around you. Praise the miracle that you yourself are. For the heart's goal is the success that does not rust or rot. Listen then to your heart and let it direct your path. For life gives you, not what you say or do, not what you amass or control, but that which you are.

As we all take responsibility for ourselves, we create a responsible government.

GOVERNMENT

Governments were created for the purpose of regulating certain human activities so that all would comply with a set of standards or laws deemed appropriate for the existence of a society. Humanity has forgotten the real understanding of divine law and the principles of life, and has found it necessary to set up artificial bodies and individuals for that regulation.

While it is admirable to aspire to an ideal of law and order, it has become a travesty that people have placed upon their government the responsibility of administering to all their needs and requirements. That is giving away one's individual sovereignty and freedom. To the degree that you are governed, you are not free. Yet you created and allowed this to happen by not taking full responsibility for yourselves. There is no blame in this. It is only an experience.

You have tried to make government do things for you that it cannot efficiently do. You have learned a valuable lesson, so there is no failure here. The time has come to cease any blame or victimization, and to take back the rights and powers that were surrendered. And if you will take the time to connect with your inner wisdom, then the true government of your affairs will be found and understood quite naturally within. As you learn, express and apply love, you will not need to be governed.

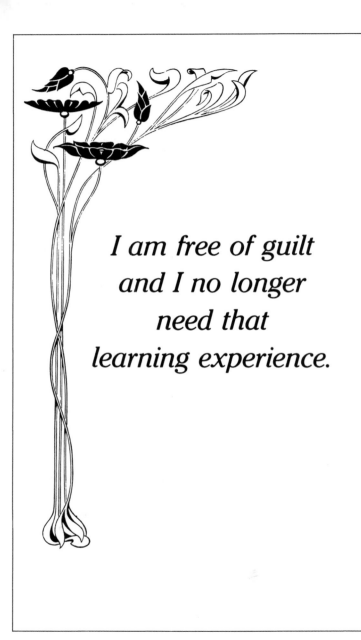

*I am free of guilt
and I no longer
need that
learning experience.*

GUILT

Guilt is a feeling based on the thought that you did something wrong. It is a feeling of separation from your freedom to be as you choose to be. You take on the burden of guilt whenever you leave the thought of love. If you would truly abide in love, you would not commit deeds whose fruit is guilt. Life has never judged you and you are forever forgiven.

Listen to your heart, for therein lie the answers to all your questions. Guilt is your own creation, and you simply wanted it for the experience. Allow it, and only one experience is enough to own the wisdom.

When you are attuned to the creation of perfection, all guilt shall pass away. In the eternity of life, all have been forgiven of any act where they presume to have been in error. In the moment you accept forgiveness you begin to create a new life with a divine purpose free from guilt and regret.

Growth is retarded in regret, compassion dissipated in anger, and life stagnated in guilt. But truth begets truth, and in love, life blossoms forth in an eternal radiant beauty.

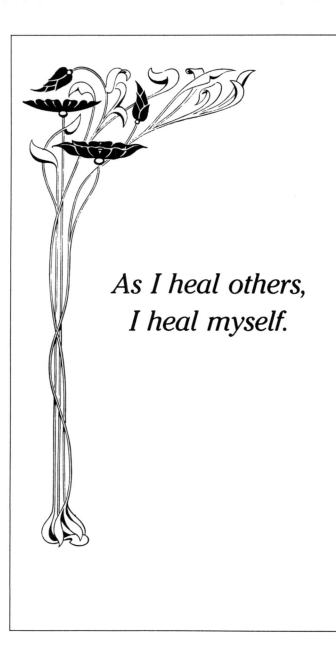

As I heal others,
I heal myself.

HEALING

ealing is the art of expressing love for your brothers and sisters in life. When you encourage them, you heal their wounds of fear.

When you forgive their errors, you heal their imagined guilt.

When you give to their bodily needs, you heal their seeming lack.

When you give them compassion, you heal their anguish and dread.

When you embrace them, you heal their sense of aloneness.

When you teach them truth, you heal their ignorance.

When you share with them a beauty in creation, you heal their perception.

When you praise them just for their being, you heal their self-esteem.

When you give them love from your heart, you heal their separation from life.

When you do these things for another, you do it for yourself, and you shall also be healed.

*I hear the voice
of my
inner wisdom.*

HEARING

Your ability to hear depends upon your willingness to do so. There are many who are resistant to truth, especially to hearing the truth about themselves. That is because they hear in terms of self-judgment or criticism. Problems with physical hearing result from rigidity in thinking, stubbornness in manner, and inflexibility in living. You hear only what you want to hear or what you are ready to hear. Rarely do you allow yourself to truly hear truth.

There is another form of hearing to which you are just beginning to become aware. It is the voice of your inner wisdom. It does not speak to you in words of criticism or judgment. It speaks to you in silence through gentle urges to use words and activities of greater love and joy. That still small voice is what can guide you through the tempest to safe harbor, direct you to create works of art, inspire you to speak lovingly and with eloquence, and assist you to always express from love and compassion. Listen with your heart, not with your mind. It has always been there, waiting for you to be quiet enough for long enough to recognize it. And if you listen, it will be music to your ears.

*I connect with
my higher self
and my life is filled
with miracles.*

HIGHER SELF

The soul and the higher self are aspects of who you really are that you have lost contact with at the conscious level. They are not separate from you, but parts of you that are far more perceptive and powerful. It is through the power of the soul and higher self that the desires of the conscious self are actualized and brought into experience.

Wisdom to the soul is the emotion experienced in life. That is one of the reasons why it is so important not to deny your feelings and emotions, but to allow, acknowledge, validate and understand them. Many of you have been denying for far too long what you really feel about the experiences of your life. Experiences that keep repeating themselves often represent lessons unlearned or wisdom that has been denied.

The soul and higher self communicate with the conscious self through desire and emotion. The still small voice of the higher self is that gentle urge, often to do something just for the pure fun of it. But the conscious self judges on the basis of the limited perspectives of appearances gained through the physical senses. They are but a narrow spectrum of all that life contains. The soul and higher self perceive a much broader spectrum of possibilities, and so their communication to the conscious self is based on a much greater knowing. By connecting with your higher self and following its guidance, your experience of life is enhanced and filled with love, joy, happiness and miracles.

*I express compassion
and understanding
for those who
are homeless.*

HOMELESSNESS

The experience of homelessness has many causes. Some are rebelling against the traditional values of humanity to seek more freedom. Some have experienced loss so that they will learn gratitude for what they have. Some want humanity to take care of them rather than be responsible for themselves. Others simply do not feel that they have a home in the callousness and coldness they experience from life.

No matter what the cause of homelessness may be, it offers the rest of humanity the opportunity to express more love, compassion and understanding. If humanity continues to judge the homeless, to deny their existence or to avoid dealing with the issues they represent, then the risk is that more will become homeless in order to get the understanding.

The homeless are not a burden. They are symbolic of areas in the human experience that are diseased and needing love. They are a gift that will assist humanity in expanding the consciousness of love and the desire for more freedom. In this time of great change, life can frown upon you as easily as it may smile, no matter how much you think you have protected yourself with the materiality you have accumulated.

With humility
and love
I give service
to life.

HUMILITY

*H*umility is the quiet wisdom which loves and accepts its place of service in the knowingness that all things and activities are the gifts of life. Humility does not seek self-recognition, does not promote itself in lofty righteousness, nor make vain displays of its justification. Its reward is within, for it is part of the essence of life.

Those who embrace humility shall find wisdom in their hearts, for humility is the soul's knowing of its oneness with all life. To be humble is to set aside the self. To become humble one often must endure pain. But through the pain come compassion, wisdom, and growth. Pain may be a great teacher, but humility quickens the heart to acceptance. Humility removes vanity and pride, and widens the door to the heart that seeks to know and express love.

I allow myself
to express
my joyous
inner child.

INNER CHILD

The inner child is that part of you that is playful and imaginative, loving and spontaneous, creative and adventurous, knowing and feeling, and yet humble and filled with awe and gratitude. The inner child trusts life and the universe to provide for what it asks. It does not sit around doing nothing, for it is too busy living life and doing what brings it joy.

The inner child has great wisdom. It knows what would truly be joyful. It does not think in terms of limitation and it does not judge anyone for their differences. Yesterday does not cause it regret, nor does it worry about a tomorrow that is not here. The great power of love within which is able to solve and dispel all seeming problems is its ally and friend. This is who you really are when the faces of fear and limitation are removed. Allow that love from within to come forth and once again be that child. You can have a grand adventure of discovery and play with life again. Doesn't it sound like fun?!

Inspiration allows me to create with joy.

INSPIRATION

*I*nspiration is the life force energy that tells you how and what to create from joy. Inspiration is the feeling of your connection to the divine guidance within. You frequently want to feel and express greater joy. You do so through the energies of inspiration and creativity. Your aliveness is enhanced and expanded any time you create from joy. Your love of life is your openness to that energy.

Your mind and intellect sometimes embrace thoughts that you cannot do what you see others doing. That is not the truth of who you are. If you would be willing to surrender that limited thought to the possibility that you can also receive inspiring guidance, then no limitation can restrict you for long. Through your imagination you will connect with solutions to even the most difficult of challenges. You are defeated only if you give up. The one who says "*I can't*," never will. But if you say "*I think I can*," the universe will show you the way.

*I know myself
and I am honest
with myself
and others.*

INTEGRITY

Integrity is a state of consciousness in which you are self-aware and honest. There are many who think that one must exhibit perfection to have integrity. Perfection is an ideal to which one may aspire, but honesty and integrity are the qualities through which that ideal may be actualized.

In your own aspiration for greatness and perfection, have kindness and compassion for yourself and others. Awareness and enlightenment bring the knowledge of all truth, not just of what you approve or agree. When you know yourself, you will find your divinity and your limitations. Have the courage and the love to accept them both. Do aspire to express your divinity, but do so with humility and gratitude. Do not deny or repress limitation. Have the honesty and integrity to see and allow it. You cannot get to where you want to go if you do not first know where you are.

*I find joy
and laughter
in this moment.*

JOY

oy and laughter are the music of children, the mind's release of all to the care and direction of life. It is the lifting of your thoughts and emotions beyond self-imposed limitations and fears to that special peace within. Laughter is the heart's expression when joy is allowed to reside. And joy is the destiny of the soul that loves life.

And how may one find the experience of joy? It is by being in the present moment, and not in yesterday or tomorrow. It is the recognition of life as a playful exploration of discovery rather than a serious set of circumstances. It is the knowing and understanding of the principles of life not as rules and regulations, but in the freedom of truth and simple being. It is in the exhilaration of giving love to all of life's blessed creations, and not in any judgment or condemnation. In this, one becomes as a child without fear, without judgments, with only laughter and joy while playing with life.

*I replace judgment
with compassion
and understanding.*

JUDGMENT

$\mathcal{J}$t is a great responsibility to assume that you have reached such a point of perfection as to be worthy of judging your own actions or those of another, for then you proclaim that you have no error thinking. Your life force is perfection, for it is the divine creation of the universe. Yet your thoughts and emotions are your own creation, and are still a limitation. You can only see in another what is within yourself. Your perception or judgment of life is the extent of your own level of awareness.

The more you become enlightened in love are you humbled by its revelations. For then you realize that whenever you judge the words or acts of another, you do also to yourself. When you are truly guided by love, all is seen in the light of compassion and understanding. Judgment ceases, and pain is replaced with peace and joy.

*The kindness
I give out
returns to me
multiplied.*

KINDNESS

Kindness is an aspect of the expression of love. When you are kind, you show to others in your words and deeds that you are caring and understanding. In being kind to yourself and others, you do not give up or surrender anything that is for your highest good. But there may be times when kindness would require you to surrender the desires of the ego to seek the higher good for all at the moment. While compassion and love may be the inner feelings, kindness is the outer activity and manifestation.

There is a poise and a calmness in the expression of kindness that assists in eliminating the stress of expectation. There is a feeling of gratitude that results from knowing the same kindness will return some day when you most need it. There is stability and strength in the expression of kindness, for it takes courage to cease all criticism and judgment. And there is the expansion of love within that enables miracles to come forth more easily. Do not hesitate to be kind to yourself and others. The love, compassion and awareness that result from kindness are precious jewels in the crown of your life.

*The law of love
guides my life.*

LAW

There is the law of man and there is the law of the universe. The law of man serves only his own selfish ends. But the law of the universe shall be known to all hearts, and is not remiss in its application. You have always had its understanding, though you try to deny that it exists.

Listen then to your heart as it speaks, for within the heart of each master is the wisdom of the law of love, that whatever you love you become.

See the lessons in the law of return, that whatever you give forth comes back to you multiplied.

Know that through the law of praise and blessing all your circumstances are elevated to your greater benefit.

Feel the peace in the law of silence, for in it you will find the presence of love.

Employ the law of forgiveness to all your brothers and sisters, for in the love and compassion of forgiveness shall you by grace be spared from pain.

And embrace the law of pure being to allow all things to be as they choose. In so doing you are sovereign and free.

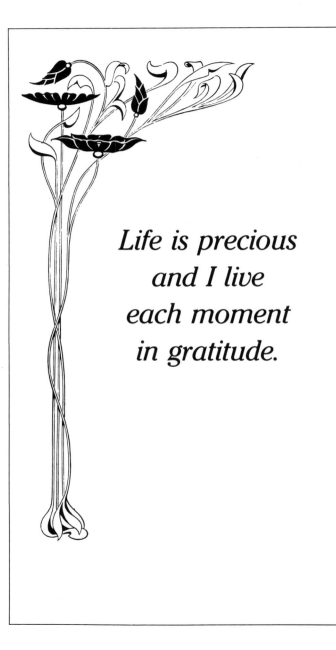

*Life is precious
and I live
each moment
in gratitude.*

LIVING

Live not in fear or hatred so that you do not create that as your experience.

Live not in judgment or condemnation, for life gives back to you what you are.

Live not in pride, self-righteousness, or arrogance, for those heights have a painful fall indeed.

Live not in greed or envy, for the universe is abundant and provides for all your needs.

Live not just for yourself, for in yourself only you will perish.

Live not in yesterdays or tomorrows, for they do not exist.

Live not without love, for in your loving prayers to life you shall find all that you desire.

Let your life be a dedication, with love from your heart, to the upliftment and encouragement of all those whom you are blessed to meet.

Live each precious moment in gratitude to life so that as life gives its unlimited self to you, you may give gloriously back to life.

And finally, remember, life only guarantees you the opportunity to participate.

Everything else is a choice.

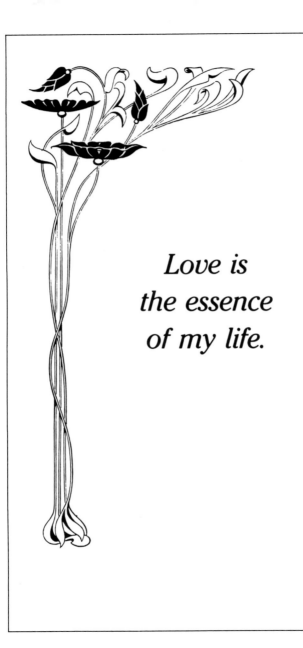

*Love is
the essence
of my life.*

LOVE

To love is to give, not merely of emotion, but of the essence of life itself. You cannot love your father or mother; you cannot love the child, friend, or mate; you cannot know of love until you taste of life. For life is the essence of being and love is the holder of life.

To love is to embrace in the grandest joy the experience of one's divinity.

To love is to feel the ecstasy in the union and unity with one's mate.

To love is to create from the perfection that the power and grace of life allows.

To love is to behold the beauty in birth and death as one.

To love is to see all the universe immersed in the caring arms of life.

To love is to know life.

And to know life is to be at one with the universe.

107

*We are united
in the presence
of love.*

MARRIAGE

Divided you were, yet united you shall be in the presence of love. And if united you seek forever to remain, then let your togetherness be as lovers, and your times apart as friends.

Let your joining be not merely in appearance, for all things change in their growth.

Let your marriage be not just in body, for then you miss the greatest of unions.

Let your days together be filled with joy, for in joy do you partake of the treasures of life.

Let your union be not in dependency, for then you lose your power to create.

Let your differences not create separation, but the awareness of your uniqueness and your synergy.

Strive to compassionately understand your differences in your oneness with life. Assist each other's heart in its quest to know love. Allow the soul to be in its own place of service and truth. And if in your wisdom you are blessed to bear fruit, give special thanks, for you have been entrusted with the most precious creation: the soul of another life.

*My faith
and love
create miracles.*

MIRACLES

Miracles are the mind's attempt to justify its denial of the principles of life. They are common events, but difficult for the doubter to understand.

Miracles abound in the quiet of peace. Miracles occur to all who believe. And miracles are indeed the experience for those who know and love life.

Yet you will rarely know or experience a miracle when you seek only to manipulate life for your own purposes. If you live in fear and confusion and do not take time for the quiet whispers of truth, you will only witness miracles in disbelief, for you sadly think it cannot happen for you.

Where there is no disbelief, doubt is vanquished. Where there is no doubt, faith accomplishes its works. Where there is faith, love is allowed to be active. When love is allowed, the mind listens to the heart, and the heart finds the wisdom of its soul. When the heart and the mind are aligned, you create in harmony with life, and all is miraculous!

*I release
the illusion
of mistakes.*

MISTAKES

You view an act or circumstance as a mistake whenever it does not produce your expectation. The concept of a mistake is an illusion of the mind. You create in thought and emotion from what you embrace as truth. Each soul, being its own master, creates its own reality. You call it a mistake whenever it is seen in negative comparison to others. From that attitude, the illusions of guilt, anger, hatred, fear, and disease are created.

There are no mistakes in life. It is only the differing levels of evolution and understanding that produce the duality in thought of a mistake. It is simply a step in remembering your higher being and destiny.

You are living your truth every moment, not just in mind and speech, but in life and in your heart. Aspire to learn the truth of your power in the love of life. Seek the wisdom in the pearls of each moment. And apply the truth you know that you may have joy. For the greatest mistake in your living is the thought that you made a mistake.

*Freedom, power
and security
are already mine.*

MONEY

*O*n your effort to amass fortunes you are desperately seeking three things: freedom, power, and security. You do not know that you have them already. They are the free gift of life and the universe with no price. But alas you have forgotten who you are. You are so attached to your illusions that you live in fear.

Money can never do for you what you can do for yourself. What greater security can you have than knowing and living the principles of life. What greater freedom can you enjoy than to live in the happiness of truth and light. And what greater power can you use than that of the life force already within?

Look around you and see the miracles you create, even with your now limited thought. Then in quiet, ponder the possibilities in a forever unlimited universe. For truly it is a truth that all things are possible to those who know and love life.

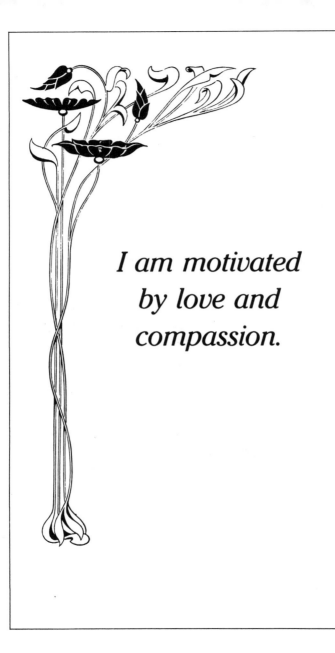

*I am motivated
by love and
compassion.*

MOTIVES

In seeking to understand the purpose of your deeds and actions, go within, for your heart always knows the answer. What you do from love seeks no other end, for love is its own reward. What you do for any other reason you often must justify to yourself to accept. If you are seeking to understand your motive, that very seeking shall tell you the answer. For when you act and give from love, your reward is in the silence of your being, and not in the expectation of verbal acknowledgement or material gain.

To understand your motive, seek to honestly know yourself. Allow what you find just to be, for you will not always be pleased at the images. See yourself growing in love and compassion, not through eyes of judgment, for then you create guilt; not through acts of condemnation, for then you become diseased; and not with feelings of anger and self-hatred, for you have already been there.

Love exactly what you are this very moment, for that is the starting point for enlightenment and change. The day shall come when your true motive to just experience life shall shine forth from within. And the light of your love will be visible to all.

*I hear the music
in all creation
and feel
its harmony.*

MUSIC

Music is the harmony in all creation.
Listen to the music of eternity, not just with your ears, but with your being.

Listen and hear the melodies of great symphonies, for they soothe away the anger and the pain.

Listen and hear the laughter of children, for they know a more joyful way to live.

Listen and hear the songs of the stars, for they tell you of eternity.

Listen to the whispers of the wind, for great spirits ride its playful tunes.

Listen to the choirs of the angels, for they speak of re-birth into the light.

And listen to the anthems of your heart, for it is the voice of life.

Listen and hear all that is around and within, for the music and harmony of creation sings of the truth of your divinity and your eternity.

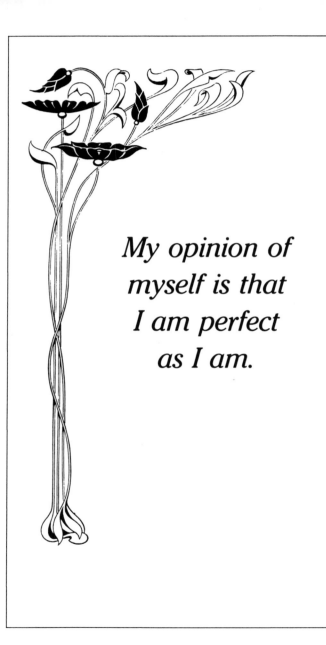

My opinion of myself is that I am perfect as I am.

OPINIONS

An opinion is simply another form of judgment. Be not dismayed or concerned by what others may think or say of you. Their perspective is limited by their own fear, anger, and judgment which are only reflections of what they feel about themselves. They cannot know you if they judge and condemn you, for then they condemn and judge the perfection in life. They cannot know life if they do not love all its manifestations. And they cannot live life in joy if they fear to see themselves in the mirrors of life. If they would truly know themselves, they would see, allow, and love the divinity in all creation.

The only opinion of value is what you have concerning your own self. You create your reality from your attitudes and beliefs about yourself. Therefore, learn to live lovingly with yourself and all creation. No matter what you do or where you go, your opinions about yourself will accompany you. When you accept yourself just as you are, without judgment or condemnation, but rather in love, great changes will occur effortlessly. And your external reality will reflect all of your loving thoughts and opinions.

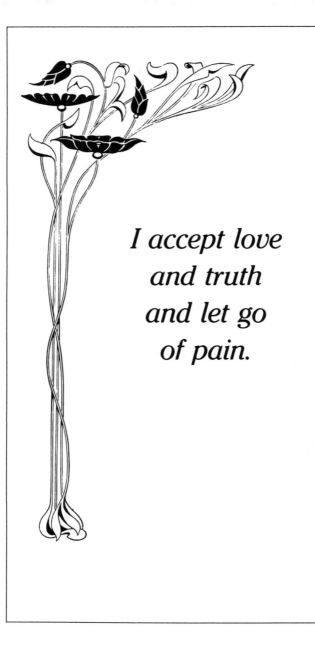

*I accept love
and truth
and let go
of pain.*

PAIN

Pain in body or emotion is a statement of being alive. The pain of an experience is often the mind's resistance to change. You endure pain because of the willful denial of truth and a lack in awareness of the gifts contained in the simple observance of life. Yet without pain you would not strive to grow and to understand, and would likely die in complacency.

Without pain there would be no incentive to seek truth. Without truth there would be no awareness. Without awareness there would be no understanding. Without understanding there would be no wisdom. Without wisdom there would be no growth. And without growth there would be no life, and all would cease to exist.

You create the pain you endure for its lessons. Even though you have come far and are worthy of praise, you have much to learn in your quest for truth. Give thanks for the lessons, even if they bring pain. Bless each circumstance as an opportunity to learn and gain wisdom. Become supple and flow with life. Then the urging from your heart and soul to seek love and truth will set you free from all pain.

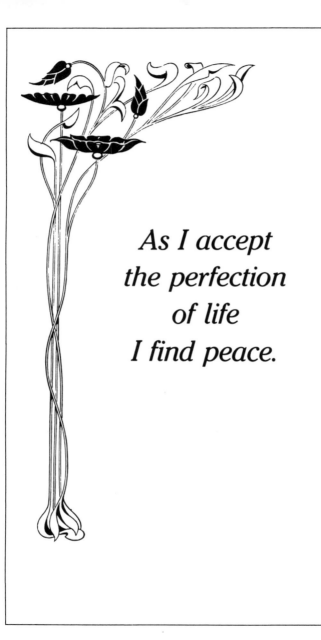

*As I accept
the perfection
of life
I find peace.*

PEACE

You desire peace. You even wage war in its name. But you shall never experience real peace as long as there is division, polarity, judgment, or condemnation. Peace does exist, it is a truth. And you bring it into your being and reality by allowing in unconditional love.

The great movement now in behalf of peace is destined for a higher understanding, because if its advocates do not have love within, then they must experience the duality of their creation in needing to fight for it. Peace will come, but not in a movement. It will come from within each heart, and without speaking of itself or advocating its necessity, without proclaiming its existence or its polarity. It will just be.

How can you know if you are peaceful within? If you can look upon all your brothers and sisters, and see beyond the flesh to the heart and soul, even to the perfection of life within, and see nothing more, and if you can look upon and respect all creation as alive, then you are allowing in unconditional love, and you will have peace within. As within, so without, and peace will manifest as your reality.

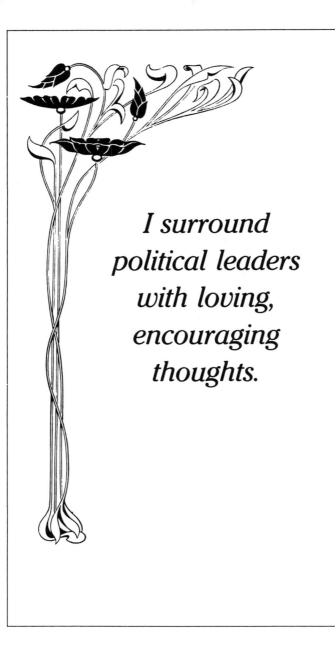

I surround political leaders with loving, encouraging thoughts.

POLITICIANS

Those who serve you in politics have placed themselves in a most precarious and scrutinized position.

Do not expect them to be perfect. They are no better than you. But do encourage them to exemplify greater honesty and integrity.

Do not expect them to keep all their promises. They are often motivated from ego even more than you. But do inspire them to speak justly and with compassion.

Do not glorify them or put them on a pedestal. You will be very disappointed when they fall from their heights and you see them for who they really are. But do demand their aspiration to live higher principles.

Do not expect them to have unblemished pasts. They too are simply evolving souls who learn through experience. But do urge them to hold a brighter vision for the future and to serve tirelessly and unselfishly to create it.

Above all, send them loving and encouraging thoughts, even when they err. After all, they are your leaders.

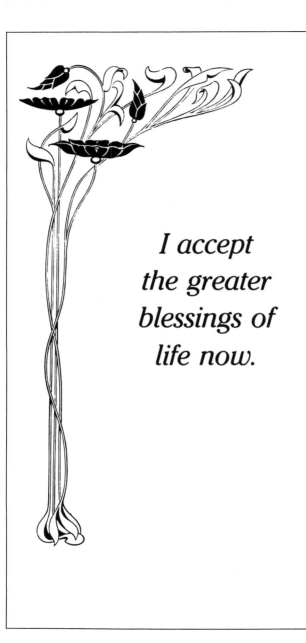

*I accept
the greater
blessings of
life now.*

POSSESSIONS

You think that you possess your things, but more often they possess you. Your thoughts and feelings are what you truly own. You can own no thing in and of itself, for it belongs to life and the universe. What you seek to possess you risk spending much futile energy in attempting to protect and retain, until finally in exhaustion you let it go. Then the wisdom of it is yours.

You may surely have what you desire, but let not the having be the end or the goal. Let it be instead a gift in the flow of life. And when the time comes that it must depart, let it do so in humble thanksgiving. For then shall you be assured of even better than what has come before.

How can you have room for the greater blessings of life if you are unwilling to let go of what you have? Life wants for you even more than you desire. Yet if you desire only for selfish motives or in a time premature, then it may likely be difficult to realize. And you are more possessed by the desire than the creator of it.

I accept the power of my thoughts and feelings.

POWER

You often ascribe the meaning of power to money, sexuality, or intellect. The day is coming when money shall pass away, when sexuality does not exist, and when knowledge is universal to all. Then what will be your power?

Your real power is your feeling. Through intense emotion you empower thought to become experience. You are the creator of your own destiny in all its manifestations.

Your power is also in the knowing of who and what you truly are in your being. It is not in a thing or purpose, for it was your power that created them. It is not in sexuality or intellect, for it was your power that defined them. And it is not in your dreams and fantasies, for it was your power that brought them into manifestation. Your power is the reality of life within as energy in motion. When this is finally understood and accepted, you will be greatly humbled in compassion and love to all creation.

*I greet everyone
as a master,
and I look for
their hidden pearls.*

PREJUDICE

One who is prejudiced towards another has not yet learned compassion or understanding, and witnesses the universe through windows narrowed by judgment and fear.

In the march of time and the growth of the soul's awareness, whatever one does not understand, one shall create and witness in one's own being. Where one does not have compassion, one shall yet experience. And whatever one hates or condemns, one shall become. It is part of the law of life.

If you find prejudice within, you need not be condemned by the law, for there are many experiences in your past and present through which you can learn and grow. You need only observe without judgment, and allow without indicting or condemning. Then the wisdom and understanding of each moment and each person allows you to bypass the need for direct experience.

If you truly seek a less painful path than prejudice, then endeavor to go through life with truth as your goal, joy as your guide, peace as your companion, laughter as your expression, and love as your being. Greet everyone as a master, for all have hidden pearls.

*In humility
I experience
my greatness.*

PRIDE

The greatness that one achieves accompanied by pride shall be lost in its own criticism, for there shall always be greater ones than those who proudly proclaim their own glory. The proud cannot be easily taught, and they learn painfully and poorly. Pride in its ignorance becomes foolish. Folly in its triteness becomes stagnant. And resistance in its decay creates disease.

Let those who are proud be wary, for their fruit is self-hatred, and the bride they court is death. Those who are humble in greatness acknowledge the source of their blessings, and seek the greater truth and love within. The proud only serve themselves, and in comparisons and judgments create the very hell they fear. But the humble serve all and seek no reward other than the love of their service. And in that service they find joy, peace, and everlasting life.

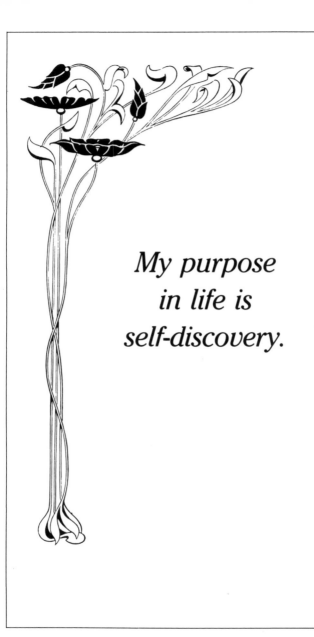

*My purpose
in life is
self-discovery.*

PURPOSE

veryone wants to feel that their lives have a meaning and purpose. But there are times when that meaning seems lost amidst a cloud of confusion and rapid change. In those times when life seems to have no meaning or purpose, there is great inner growth taking place, whether it is conscious or not. It is a time to just let yourself be without the need for constant activity or diversion. One of the great lessons of the human experience is how to just be. When you learn and understand your own growth cycles, it will be easy to allow the inner its time of process, and the outer a time of rest.

The purpose of life is its own awareness. Your purpose in life is self-discovery. Your life experiences aid in the actualization of that purpose. You cooperate with your own process and timing by learning how to love yourself. In learning how to love, you also become more aware. The purpose of silence is to allow that awareness. There is all of eternity *to do*. There is only now *to be*.

*I admire and
respect all races
in my family
of humanity.*

RACE

The different races of humanity each have a purpose and gift for the others. There is much for you to learn from those who may be of different color skin. Just as you would not think of judging a person who was born on Tuesday to be better than someone born on Friday, so too cease all judgment concerning race or nationality. You are all human beings. Color as perceived by your eyes is based on a very narrow spectrum of light. You would be better off blind than to judge anything in life merely because of its appearance. You deny yourself many gifts and treasures when you do.

Your thoughts and feelings about some one or some thing is an energy that goes forth and surrounds them. You are in effect creating them to be what you think them to be by the power of your thought and belief, especially if they are not sufficiently awakened to be aware and protected from your thoughts. Your body has different cells to carry out certain functions necessary for your life. So too will you discover that each race has been given a gift to share with all others to enhance life and make it more joyful. Look only for what you can admire and respect in each other and encourage its expression. Then you will see the great value in each other and there will be no need of judgment or racial prejudice.

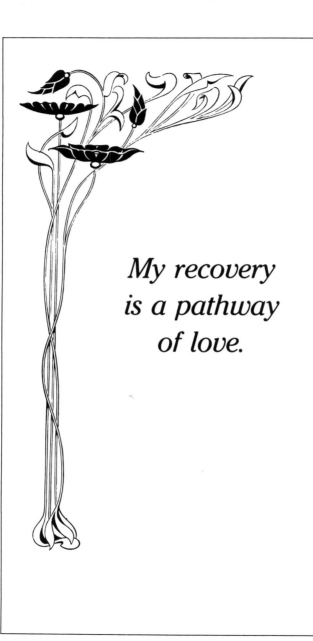

*My recovery
is a pathway
of love.*

RECOVERY

As an infant and a child, many of you did not receive the love and care you wanted and deserved. Your brain became wired with thoughts and feelings of great limitation. Later in life you began to grow and became more aware of how those limitations have caused your life to be less than joyful. Healing and changing the beliefs which resulted from early childhood experiences is the process often called recovery. It takes time. So be kind to yourself and give yourself time to gain awareness and to learn how to make different choices.

Early childhood experiences caused you to develop limited identities and defense mechanisms from the hurts you received. As a child you knew truth, but you were taught limitation. You rebelled, but were punished. You tried to express your thoughts and feelings, but they were denied and invalidated. And now you are seeking to be rid of the pain.

You begin recovery by being honest with yourself. Cease speaking negatively, but do not deny what you feel. The power of positive thought and words is wonderful, but is only a beginning. You must also change what you feel. That is most easily accomplished by surrounding yourself with friends who have been there, and who understand what you are going through and trying to heal. Then you can release the repressed emotions that have been blocking you from your joy. By making more appropriate choices, you move forward and love and respect yourself more.

141

My perfect relationship is the love of my own being.

RELATIONSHIPS

You desire to know the meaning of your relationships with your lovers and mates. What you are truly seeking is an understanding and love of yourself. No one or thing can give you happiness or fulfillment. That must come from within. For who will love you if you do not love yourself?

There is no philosophy, movement, or doctrine that can teach you greater or more quickly than that which is already within. Seek to know and express the love in your heart, the love for yourself and all creation, for in that only can you find the meaning, the understanding, and the fulfillment you desire.

Your happiness is your own responsibility. Do not depend on others to make you happy. Seek first a relationship with yourself that loves, forgives, and allows yourself to be. Only when you love what you are can you love the same in another. Compare yourself to no one, nor another to another. For each has his place in forever, and each must find his own relationship in the love of his own being.

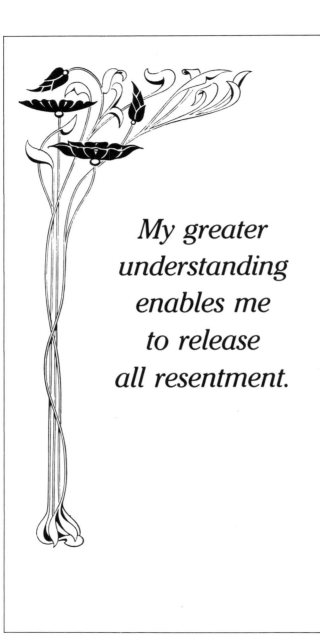

*My greater
understanding
enables me
to release
all resentment.*

RESENTMENT

Resentment is a form of judgment and hatred and one of the greatest blockages to prosperity and well-being. If you have resentment towards any person or circumstance in life, it will keep you stagnated and trapped. The anger that results causes the body to become toxic, and if held long enough contributes to disease. The cause of resentment is your attempt to force life or another person to be something they are not. You must learn to allow and you must learn how to love without expectation or condition. Otherwise you only seek to enslave life which ends up enslaving you.

Life simply is what it is. Your thoughts and feelings about life create your experience of it. To free yourself from resentment is to see life from more than one perspective. Every moment you are doing the best that you can. And so is everyone else. When you truly understand this, you will no longer need to judge or resent anything. It is only the vain and limited identity of your ego that feels threatened or resentful. And when you no longer need that identity, you will be free from resentment.

*In the heart
of life
I find only love.*

RIGHT AND WRONG

To speak of right and wrong is to examine the two faces of a coin. It is a single coin, only a duality of perspectives. When you accept that a coin is only a coin, then you shall know the difference. What is hate, but unlearned love? And a lie, but a twist of the truth? Yet all have their story to tell of what life is and isn't to them.

Who then is right or who is wrong? Truth is merely relative to the perspective of the observer. Right and wrong, good and bad are polarities of judgment in the mind. No one is truly worthy and wise enough to be the judge of another.

Right and wrong are the creations of a polarized mind, and not the loving observation of life simply as it is. Only in the mind of humanity can there ever be anything less than the perfection of life. In the heart of life there is only love.

My sexual expression is a celebration of my wholeness.

SEXUALITY

Sexual union is a joining, not only in body, but in mind, emotion and spirit. Sexual desire is the urge within to unite in wholeness and completeness those parts of yourself that you have either denied or did not know exist. You are all whole and complete as you are. Sexual expression is a celebration with another of your awareness of that wholeness.

Do not make the sexual act a mockery of the unity and love it symbolizes by seeking only physical gratification. That is a misuse of the life force that animates your body.

Do not make a god of sexuality, for then you risk becoming possessed by it and losing your free will.

Let the act of sexual union be guided and consecrated by real love and mutual respect. Then you will not create guilt.

Let your union be from already knowing your wholeness, and not from what you think you do not have.

And do not seek only to merge with the appearance of a perfect body, but do desire to join and connect with the perfect heart of love. Then in time, when the life force quite naturally moves higher in the body, you will still enjoy the company of a friend.

*I love myself
for all that
I have experienced.*

SHAME

$\mathcal{S}$hame is the feeling that there is something wrong with you. You are an evolving and growing soul. To grow and evolve you must experience life, and from that experience you gain wisdom. When you apply your wisdom, you perceive greater options and choices. If you have not had an experience, your options are vague or unknown.

No matter what it appears that one is experiencing, it is a result of the urging from the soul to know all that life contains. To do a seeming "wrong" out of ignorance is not a crime to the universe, for you live by grace. But to ignore what one knows just to satisfy some desire or lust of the ego is to forget the love and wisdom within.

Conscience is healthy shame, the reflection of wisdom to assist in making appropriate choices. But to live a life that is shame based in one's being is to say that it is wrong to learn by experience. That goes against the principles of life and keeps one in limitation. To heal the shame, love yourself for all you have experienced, and give yourself permission to learn from it.

*I see only
the perfection
in myself and
the universe.*

SICKNESS

Illness and disease are fruits of fear and hatred, and are directed at your own self. Worries and stress cause your body to revolt against itself in confusion. You often find yourself sick because you want to be. It is your lack of self-love and acceptance, and your perspective of error and guilt. You even seek love expressed in another's pity. If you continue this thinking, you only perpetuate the sickness you fear.

The greatest cause of disease is anger. The greatest cause of anger is expectation. And the greatest cause of expectation is that you do not allow in love. You expect, but are unwilling to give. You desire affection, but are unwilling to love. You seek for truth with closed eyes. And you judge without first understanding.

Eliminate fear, anger, and hatred from your being, and disease will cease to exist. Look within for your answers in the quiet peace and serenity of your heart. Accept disease as your own creation, then create it no more. See only the perfection in the universe and you will live at ease in joy, truth, and love.

*I give myself
time for quiet
and reflection.*

SILENCE

ilence is a state of being and a feeling in which you are open and willing to hear the divine guidance and wisdom from within. It does not depend on the absence of sound in your external world, but it does depend on the absence of limited thought. To quiet your mind, to have no thought, is desirable for the experience of silence. Self-awareness is revealed through silence, so there are many of you who avoid it. But self-awareness is part of the purpose of being and you cannot postpone it. Life reflects it to you at every turn.

To enter into silence, simply close your eyes and envision yourself being filled with light. This is nurturing to the heart and soul, and allows you a closer relationship with yourself. Since all your relationships depend on that foundation within, giving yourself time for quiet and reflection is vital to sustaining your sense of self and the love you have achieved. It is a time of conscious recharging of your being. If you take short but frequent times to be alone, you will likely not ever feel the need to withdraw from life. In silence you will also discover that you are never alone, for you will find your best friend.

*I speak only
what I want
to experience.*

SPEECH

Your speech often hides your true thoughts, for it is rare that you say what you think, or mean what you say. The riddles of diplomacy and tact do far more injustice in their hypocrisy than any act of simple spoken truth. Yet you fear truth because of its revelations. You do not see the divinity in all life, but rather the creations of limitation and fear. Your perceptions are clouded in dogma and belief, and what you speak is from misunderstanding.

In quiet simplicity is wisdom made known. In humble thanksgiving is the joy of life's increase. And in the compassion of love is the understanding of life. For speech is not merely in spoken words, lest you presume that your thoughts can remain hidden. For what manifests in your life is a product of your thinking.

Therefore think only what you are willing to live, for your life is most surely created in thought. Speak only what you want to experience, and only when you have its understanding. Every word you speak is the decree of the divine being that you are.

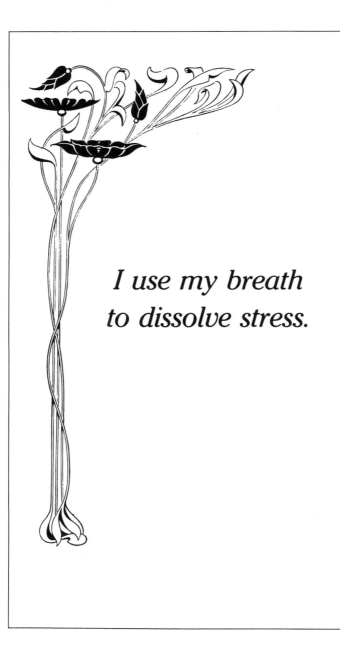

*I use my breath
to dissolve stress.*

STRESS

Stress is one of the greatest causes of disease, and a result of unrealistic expectations. Many people experience stress in their lives because they have sold out their happiness for materiality. They have so repressed the gentle urgings from the heart that even when those urgings become a roar, they still go unheeded. Many people experience job stress because they are not doing what they love. They have not learned to trust themselves or to trust life. It takes courage to be different.

Others experience stress and anxiety because they live in regret of yesterday or fear of tomorrow. Neither of those exist. Now is the only moment that is. By being more in now, you learn from your yesterdays. By being more fully in now, you increase the opportunity to create a joyful and peaceful tomorrow. And by being fully in now, time expands, joy fills the body and soul, and stress ceases to interfere with happiness.

If you are experiencing stress, a wonderful way to dissolve it is to pay attention to your breathing. If you breathe fully and deeply and are conscious of the breath, it assists you in focusing in now. By being in now, you are better able to connect with your power of choice. The choice in that moment is whether you will react to the circumstances you have created as if they had power over you, or whether you will apply your power to create differently. Honor what you feel. Then take charge of your life by choosing to focus on what you want to experience.

*My greatest
teacher
is within.*

TEACHERS

Ｏn your search for truth and understanding, do not seek the proud, for they only proclaim their own glory.

Do not seek the self-righteous who have not found love in their hearts.

Do not seek the loud and profane, for they have lost the wisdom of silence.

Do not seek those who appeal to your greed, for you shall ever be in want on tasting their fruit.

And do not seek those with evil in their minds, for they have no love for life.

Listen to the wisdom of your children, for they are closer to the heavens of your dreams.

Hearken your ears to the humble in spirit, for they have learned compassion and forgiveness.

Let your eyes witness the works of those who only serve, for they know their connections with all life.

Feel the warmth in the embrace of a friend, for true friends are a treasure and have the precious gift of love.

And let your mind connect with your heart, for the greatest teacher is within.

I allow myself
to feel
and I am safe.

TEARS

Tears are the body's mechanism for cleansing away the toxins of grief. You often repress the grief and sadness associated with loss and rejection. In these times of change and rapid evolution, it is important to realize that there will be times when you must let go of someone or something. You never lose the level of love and joy you have gained and earned. It is always waiting within to be brought forth again.

Many of you feel for the earth and its plants and animals. You weep over the seeming end of a species or way of life. Ask for comfort and healing and it will come to you. Seek out those friends who understand what you feel. If need be, allow the tears to flow in torrents. They are pearls of love. And the day will surely come when your tears will be from the great joy you feel in your heart and soul.

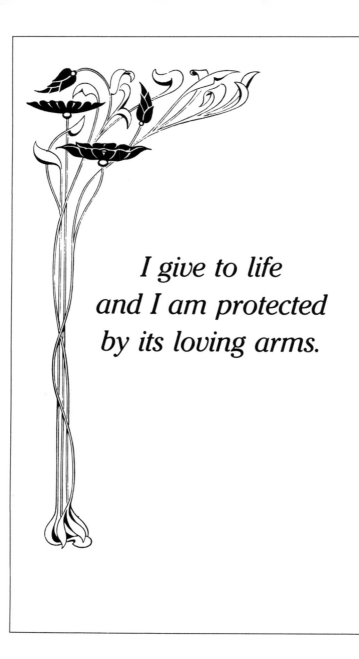

*I give to life
and I am protected
by its loving arms.*

THEFT

No one can remove from you what you own. But what do you truly possess, other than your thoughts and feelings? You think that a wrong has been done when someone takes from you. But have you not also coveted another's possessions, or envied his position in life? Have you not also desired, but been unwilling to pay the price? Who are the more true to themselves: thieves who live their thinking, or one who surreptitiously wants all, but has nothing? Theft is created in thought, and fear causes its manifestation.

No one will take from you when you are giving to life with love. Your greatest protection is within. You will feel far greater security when you learn to trust your inner self. If you do not take from life, then life will not take from you. Any time that you express kindness or love, compassion or understanding, tolerance or forgiveness, you are giving to life. And life will lovingly guide you and show you what you need to do and where you need to be to feel its protecting arms around you.

*I trust life
and I
trust myself.*

TRUST

*H*ow can you trust when you live in fear? And how can you know trust if you never seek the quiet in which it speaks? For trust is not merely the faith that moves the mountains and calms the storms. It is the essence of the truth you seek within.

To trust is to let go of the need in the mind to control life. You allow life simply to be as it is.

To trust is to know that there is a power within you that transcends the limited perspectives of the mind and intellect.

To trust is to see beyond the appearances and to embrace each joyful desire as already fulfilled.

You learn of trust when you let go of the mind's fear in its limited perception of life.

You embrace trust when you live the purpose of your uniqueness.

And you live in trust when you allow the power of the soul to create miracles.

With trust you find your place in "forever" as the master that you truly are.

*My reverence
for life
allows me to
find truth.*

TRUTH

You seek truth, but the truth you seek is a many-sided coin. You cannot learn truth in your mind only, for truth is an experience. You cannot find truth in the world, for the world is your own vain imagining. You cannot find truth in your hearts when you have not learned to love. You cannot know truth in your soul, when you have no reverence for life. And you cannot be in truth if you live in fear.

When you no longer judge in polarizations of right and wrong, you will have found a path to truth. When you can hear the symphony in silence, you have heard the music of truth. When you find the meaning in a blade of grass, you have touched the hem of truth. When you soar like the birds in the air, you shall find the freedom of truth. When you are no longer divided, you shall be in the presence of truth. And when you no longer seek it, truth shall find you.

*I am willing
to see
the divinity
in all life.*

VISION

Physical vision is indicative of your willingness to see yourself and life as it is. You experience difficulties in vision when there are aspects of your life you do not want to see. Vision is also symbolic of your understanding of what you have experienced in life.

Your imagination is the inner sight that allows you to see and create greater possibilities for yourself and others. Those who aspire to higher ideals for humanity you call "visionaries." They see a better future, but not always the first steps necessary to get there. Others see only problems in their lives and have difficulty recognizing how they were created or how to change them.

To have better vision both physically and spiritually, change your perception about life. Change is allowed and loved into being. If change is forced, it is like a rubber band that has been stretched. It may likely return to the way it was. To lovingly see life as a process of growth and evolution is to embrace the opportunity for positive change that is both permanent and joyful. See yourself and others as divine and your vision will become perfect.

By applying love,
we can all
live in peace.

WAR

Old men jealous of lost youth often send their sons to war. Those filled with greed and lust, who never have enough, seek to enslave and impoverish the just. Women weep for their husbands and for what might have been. There never was a war that benefitted humanity, for the lesson of war's futility has not been learned.

It is an irony that you feel you must fight for peace. No one truly wins in war. There is only loss and destruction, shattered dreams and broken homes. And yet there are still those who glorify its pain. With no feeling or conscience they say it is "a job to be done." They even call themselves "human" while celebrating the victory of another's death. Where is the love in all of this?

War is a sad circumstance for humanity because it has not yet learned to love. And sadder still, the greatest technological advances have been motivated from humanity's desire to destroy. The call of evolution is for humanity to seek an alternative to war, for the next battle may be its last. That alternative is to love one's self, to love one's neighbors, and to love and understand all humanity. In applying love, you can live in peace.

I am enriched by giving of my talents and abilities.

WEALTH

You long for palaces of gold and beds of satin, feasts and revelries and wine without end. But that is often merely the lust of your mind. Within you is a seed of truth that must grow. It is the heart's longing for love, and the soul's thirst for life. No act or thing can satiate that desire other than the quiet discovery of the real truth within. Things are but illusions, symbols at best of what you truly seek.

When you find and live that truth, great shall be your reward. For richness is within you in the love and joy you feel for life. What you give to your brothers and sisters you give to yourself. What you give to life shall be returned to you in abundance. What you give is really yourself. But if in fear your purpose is only to take from life, then what you take shall in time be taken from you.

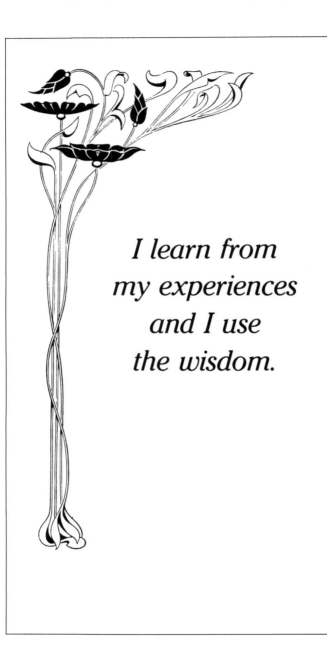

*I learn from
my experiences
and I use
the wisdom.*

WISDOM

*W*isdom is the knowing in the heart and soul of what is loving and compassionate. It is not found in the rational terms of the mind or the intellect, for they are but tools in the expression of one's personality and ego. Nor is wisdom described as the right thing to do, for in allowing without judgment there is no right or wrong.

Wisdom to the soul is the emotion experienced in the duration called time.

It is acquired simply in allowing the feeling in the experiences of life.

It is expressed in one's silence, while all around is the noise of those lost in confusion.

It is seen in one's loving humble service, while others complain of their dull fate and unhappiness.

It is heard from the mouth of a child who has not yet succumbed to fear and limitation.

It is remembered in having compassion for your brothers and sisters.

And it is lived in the surrender of the ego to the higher knowing within.

Wisdom is the gift from the soul for those who love life.

*My work is
the loving service
I give to life.*

WORK

When you choose your work, let it be from the heart of love, and not the mind of fear. That which is done from the heart seeks not vanity or pride, for it has its own reward in the joy within and the silence of the universe.

When you set out to do the tasks of a day, let those efforts be guided with the same joy, for then are the fruits multiplied and pain diminished. When your work is seen through eyes filled with joy and a heart flowing in love, tasks are accomplished in the flowing harmony and ease of peace.

When you speak of burdens, you lose touch with the purpose for life. No task is painful or burdensome when you truly love and value the opportunity to serve life. Life will never require of you any more than it is willing to give. For in love, work becomes play, and you become as a child on a grand adventure of discovery.

*I am worthy
and loved
simply because
I exist.*

WORTHINESS

Your thoughts and feelings concerning your worthiness are often equated to productivity. The universe smiles upon you, not for any task you may perform, though when you work from love you give to life, and shall enjoy its reward. Life gives of itself to you, not for what you may say, but simply for your being. And though you speak with eloquence the truths you know, your speech often hides your unknown fears.

You are always loved by life, not for your thoughts and feelings, but because you are the expression of love. And whether you rise in harmony with the eagles or wallow in the quagmire of seeming wretchedness, your thoughts and feelings are only tools for creation.

Your worth and worthiness are simply in your being. Attach no significance to the outward appearance, for in judgment you are better off blind. Do not give your dominion away in the words of another, for you are your own master and were better deaf than to clutch another's speech as the truth when your own truth lies waiting within for discovery. And do not allow your possessions to own you, for you are more free with nothing than to be bound by the illusions of materiality. You are worthy just because you exist.

*I am far
greater
than I
ever knew.*

YOU

You who have read these words are expanded. Whether any of this is your truth or will become your truth depends only on your willingness to allow greater possibilities in your life. You are blessed. You are divine. You are a far greater being than you have perhaps ever considered.

You are a spiritual being. No matter what your human life may be or become, it is only an experience. It is not who you are. Find out more about who you really are. Be who you really are. It is the greatest gift you could ever give or receive.

Let the journey in this life be a joyful experience of discovery. Let life be a playground for change and evolution. Laugh as often as you can. Let your tears cleanse away any grief. You have a very important reason for being here. And each person's reason is unique. Enjoy your differences and your uniqueness. Be in love and be in now.

NOTES

NOTES

NOTES

NOTES

NOTES

NOTES

NOTES